中英双语版
企鹅经典 名人大发现

斯蒂芬·霍金

[美] 吉姆·吉列奥蒂 (Jim Gigliotti) ◎著 [美] 格雷戈里·科普兰 (Gregory Copeland) ◎绘 高榕◎译

Who Was Stephen Hawking?

CNS 湖南科学技术出版社 小博集 BOOKY KIDS
·长沙·

著作权合同登记号：字18-2024-202

图书在版编目（CIP）数据

名人大发现. 斯蒂芬·霍金 : 汉英对照 /（美）吉姆·吉列奥蒂（Jim Gigliotti）著 ; 高榕译 ; （美）格雷戈里·科普兰（Gregory Copeland）绘. -- 长沙 : 湖南科学技术出版社，2025. 1. --（企鹅经典）. -- ISBN 978-7-5710-3273-9

Ⅰ. H319. 4

中国国家版本馆CIP数据核字第20245Z71V2号

上架建议：科普读物

QI'E JINGDIAN · MINGREN DA FAXIAN：ZHONG-YING SHUANGYU BAN SIDIFEN HUOJIN

企鹅经典·名人大发现：中英双语版　斯蒂芬·霍金

著　　者：［美］吉姆·吉列奥蒂（Jim Gigliotti）
绘　　者：［美］格雷戈里·科普兰（Gregory Copeland）
译　　者：高　榕
出 版 人：潘晓山
责任编辑：刘　竞
策划出品：李　炜　张苗苗　文赛峰
策划编辑：马　瑄
特约编辑：杜佳美
营销编辑：付　佳　杨　朔　周晓茜
装帧设计：利　锐
内文排版：金锋工作室
出　　版：湖南科学技术出版社
（湖南省长沙市芙蓉中路416号　邮编：410008）
网　　址：www.hnstp.com
印　　刷：三河市航远印刷有限公司
经　　销：新华书店
开　　本：875 mm × 1230 mm 1/32
字　　数：109千字
印　　张：5.25
版　　次：2025年1月第1版
印　　次：2025年1月第1次印刷
书　　号：ISBN 978-7-5710-3273-9
定　　价：22.00元

若有质量问题，请致电质量监督电话：010-59096394　　团购电话：010-59320018

目　录

Contents

谁是斯蒂芬·霍金？

霍金小时候最想要的就是一辆玩具火车。但那时英国处在 20 世纪 40 年代中期，正值第二次世界大战时期，玩具厂并不生产玩具，而是忙于支援战争。玩具厂忙着给士兵们制造飞机和炸弹，所以霍金很难找到一辆玩具火车。

于是在霍金三岁的时候，霍金的父亲给他做了一辆木制火车，但霍金并不认为那是真的火车。他必须推着火车，火车才会往前开动。后来，霍金的父亲设法找到了一辆上发条的火车。霍金转动发条，火车就会自己往前开动，但这仍然不是他想要的火车。

霍金真正想要的是一辆电动火车，里面的零部件是可以活动的。他想研究火车是如何运转的——是什么让火车开动起来，又是什么让火车停了下来。后来，等他

再大一点的时候，他就拿出自己银行账户里所有的钱，给自己买了一列电动火车。这就更接近他想要的那种火车了！

霍金很快就着手研究更大的物件。他开始制作飞机模型。后来，他又开始制作玩具船。他并不在意这些模型和玩具的外观，相反，他对它们的运转原理更感兴趣。有时他会把这些模型和玩具拆开。尽管他不太擅长把它们重新组装起来，但这并不重要。因为他想研究各种零件是如何相互作用的。

等到他十几岁的时候，霍金开始思考更大的事物是如何运转的——非常大的事物，譬如宇宙。霍金想知道：宇宙的起源是什么？宇宙会变大吗？会变小吗？宇宙会不会有一天走向终结？

这些都是重大问题！霍金一生都在思考这些重大问题，无论发生什么事都无法阻止他继续思考。即便他身患疾病，大半辈子都只能坐在轮椅上，即便他不能说话，后来还完全不能动弹，这些都无法阻止他。

相反，霍金战胜了病魔的挑战，成为一位物理学家。物理学是一门研究物质（万物由此构成）和能量的科学。研究物理学的人会仔细观察物质和能量是如何在空间和时间中运动的。

成年之后，霍金一直都在思考这些重大问题。他写了关于黑洞、宇宙起源等各种问题的文章和书。他是一位著名的科学家，也是一位重要的思想家，激励着全世界的人。

第一章

开端

1939 年，第二次世界大战在欧洲爆发，弗兰克·霍金和伊索贝尔·霍金当时还住在英国伦敦。敌对阵营的德国在战时对伦敦进行了猛烈轰炸。伦敦的许多地方都成了废墟。霍金夫妇的家没有受到袭击，但有一枚炸弹就落在离他们家不远的街上。

20世纪40年代初，伊索贝尔怀上了霍金，她一度搬到了英国牛津。牛津距离伦敦约六十英里[①]，相对来说安全多了。牛津是牛津大学的所在地，那里没有军队，也没有重要的工厂，因此并没有成为德国人的攻击目标。

1942年1月8日，霍金在这座没有硝烟的城市顺利降生。这一天恰巧是意大利物理学家伽利略逝世三百周年忌日。霍金长大后成为一位物理学家，他常开玩笑说这确实有一定的意义。但他也承认，还有成千上万的婴儿也在这一天出生，但他们长大后并没有成为著名的科学家！

弗兰克在大学主修医学，是一位热带病专家。他和妻子伊索贝尔住在伦敦的海格特，那里住着许多科学家。

霍金是弗兰克和伊索贝尔的第一个孩子。1943年，他们有了一个女儿，取名玛丽。

---

① 英里：英美制长度单位。1英里≈1.609千米。

伽利略·加利莱伊（1564—1642）

伽利略有时被誉为“现代物理学之父”。在他生活的时代，人们认为较重的物体比较轻的物体下落得更快。但伽利略发现，运动中的物体都以相同的加速度下落。

伽利略在许多学科上都是专家。他是天文学家和数学家，同时还是哲学家和工程师。

作为一位罗马天主教徒，他认为地球绕着太阳旋转，这激怒了教会领袖。当时，大多数人都认为太阳是绕着地球旋转的。1633 年，伽利略被判犯有异端罪，意味着他违背了教会教义。他被软禁在家中，度过了生命的最后九年。

1946 年，霍金夫妇迎来了他们的二女儿菲莉帕，霍金十四岁时，他们收养了一个名叫爱德华的男婴。

1950 年，他们举家搬到了距海格特以北约二十英里的圣奥尔本斯。弗兰克在位于米尔希尔的国家医药研究院担任了一个重要职位。米尔希尔地处伦敦郊区，对他来说，搬家之后上下班会更方便一些。

在圣奥尔本斯居住时，霍金一家有时在一众邻居间显得格外引人注目。八岁的霍金认为，这是因为住在圣奥尔本斯的科学家没有住在海格特的科学家多。事实的确如此，但让霍金一家显得与众不同的事情可能不止

于此。

例如，他们开着一辆二战前的老式伦敦计程车在城里兜风。孩子们坐在车里，感觉尴尬极了。为了不让朋友们看到自己坐车经过，他们都躲在宽敞的后座！不过大家都知道这是谁家的车。

霍金一家还买了一辆旧的大篷车，也就是马车。他们把马车停在附近城镇的一块田野里，打算以后就来这里度假。暑假时，孩子们睡在大篷车里，大人们就在旁边搭一顶军用帐篷。

霍金一家住在家里的时候也不走寻常路。家里到处都是书。孩子们甚至在晚饭时间读书。

家里有很多书架，都放得满满当当。即便看起来已经放不下了，还是会有更多的书堆在原来的那一排排书上面，或者塞到前面。

毫不奇怪，霍金是有点安静的。他经常独自一人玩。有时，亲戚们会发现他正盯着天空，思考着远大的想法。

不过，霍金并不羞于表达自己的观点，他还交了很多朋友。要是他的朋友们来家里玩，一家人就会在晚餐时间放下书本，聊聊天。他的小伙伴们对霍金一家讨论的宗教或政治等大人之间的话题感到非常惊讶。霍金曾说：“家是一个让我的思想不断接受挑战的地方。”

第二章

学生时代

小时候，霍金喜欢玩棋盘游戏。不过，像大富翁这样的游戏对他来说很快就变得无聊至极，无法满足他活跃的思维。于是，霍金和朋友一起自制了棋盘游戏。霍金最喜欢的是一种非常复杂的战争游戏。因为霍金在游戏中加入了非常多的规则，所以这种游戏能玩好几个小时。

他的妹妹玛丽后来回忆说，霍金非常好胜。

无论玩什么游戏，他都想赢。英国的跳棋就是国际跳棋。霍金每次玩跳棋都能赢玛丽，只有一次输了。玛丽终于赢了他一次之后，霍金就再也不玩跳棋了，开始玩国际象棋。玛丽跟霍金玩国际象棋的时候从来没赢过他！

虽然霍金非常聪明，但他直到八岁才学会阅读，而且很少在学校学习。他的作业并不工整，字也写得很难看。霍金对记忆事实没什么兴趣，但能够轻易掌握各种概念和理念。

等到十几岁的时候，霍金和他的朋友们一起制造了一台电脑。这台电脑和我们现在的笔记本电脑完全不一样，大约有冰箱那么大。他们用所有能找到的零件制造了这台电脑，甚至还用了旧钟表的零件。

虽然这台电脑只能解决最基本的问题，但当时还是20世纪50年代末，霍金已然走在了时代的前列！

阿尔伯特·爱因斯坦

事实上，因为霍金实在是太聪明了，所以他的朋友们都叫他“爱因斯坦”。这个名字源自著名物理学家阿尔伯特·爱因斯坦。但在课堂上，霍金可不是爱因斯坦。与同年级的其他同学相比，他只是一个普通学生。他后来开玩笑说：“我觉得那个班级的同学可真是太聪明了！”

在学校里，霍金经常感到无聊。物理对他来说太简单了。对一个思维如此超前的人来说，解题方法是显而易见的。像化学这样的科目要有趣得多。在化学课上，他可以弄清楚不同元素之间是如何相互作用的。有些元

素之间能产生很好的化学反应，而有些元素相互作用则会导致爆炸，这有趣极了！

霍金的父母都毕业于牛津大学，他们希望霍金也能就读牛津大学。但由于霍金在圣奥尔本斯学校里成绩平

平，他不能保证自己被牛津大学录取。

霍金在大学里读什么专业也是个问题。弗兰克希望儿子能够子承父业，学习医学。但霍金对生物学或当医生并不感兴趣。他想主修数学，但牛津大学学院没有开设数学专业。于是，霍金选择了物理学。

霍金的面试表现相当出色，物理笔试成绩更是令人赞叹，几乎是满分，令牛津大学的老师们惊叹不已！霍金就这样拿到了牛津大学的录取通知书。

1959 年秋，年仅十七岁的霍金开始了在牛津大学的学习生涯。他的同学们很快就看出他非常聪明，人也很风趣。不过，他还是花了一点时间才和其他同学打成一片。几乎所有的同学都比他大，其中一些人比他大好几岁。

为了多结识一些人，霍金在大学二年级的时候加入了大学学院赛艇队。虽然他很瘦，也不是很强壮，但他还是在一堆体格健壮的桨手中找到了自己的一席之地。他担当舵手，也就是坐在赛艇的一端指挥桨手和掌舵的小个子。

牛津大学

牛津大学坐落于英国牛津，是世界上现存的第二古老的大学（最古老的大学是意大利的博洛尼亚大学，始建于1088年）。牛津大学的建校时间没有官方数据，但据说最早可追溯到1096年。

牛津大学由三十八所不同的学院组成。每所学院都有各自的教师和活动。霍金就读的大学学

院是三十八所学院中历史最为悠久的。

世界上许多优秀的学者都曾就读于牛津大学，其中包括几十位诺贝尔奖得主。许多世界领导人也曾在牛津大学就读，包括二十七位英国首相，还有美国总统比尔·克林顿。克林顿于20世纪60年代末在牛津大学学院学习了一年，之后进入耶鲁大学法学院学习。

霍金花了一段时间才掌握当舵手的窍门。由于牛津镇的泰晤士河河道狭窄，赛艇队参加的其实是“撞击”比赛。在撞击比赛中，赛艇在开始时相互之间的距离相等。他们要奋力划快一点，既要撞开前面的赛艇，又要

避免被后面的赛艇撞到。

第一次参加比赛的时候，霍金按规定指挥赛艇冲出起跑线，但船舵钩住了缆绳。（霍金所在的队伍立即被取消了比赛资格。）还有一次，他不知怎的指挥自己所在的

赛艇与另一艘赛艇迎面相撞。（他表示这并不是自己的错。）他通常都是在赛艇或队友的桨受损的情况下才指挥

赛艇往回开。（霍金承认："我的舵手生涯相当糟糕。"）

尽管如此，霍金还是很享受在河上划赛艇的感觉。

他跟赛艇队的很多队员都成了朋友。队员们也对他的聪明幽默印象深刻。他说："参加赛艇队还让我发现了我在牛津最喜欢的消遣方式之一，那就是参加聚会！"

也许聚会有点太多了。就读牛津大学的第二年，霍金花在参加社交活动上的时间远比他花在学习上的时间要多。他后来估算过，在牛津大学的三年里，他花在学习上的时间大约有一千个小时。一千个小时听起来似乎很多，但算起来平均每天不到一小时！其实霍金花在学习上的时间是非常少的，虽然他就读于牛津大学这样一所充满挑战的学校，学习的也是物理这样一门难度很大的课程。

霍金经常逃课，还因此背上了“很难相处”的名声。有一次他和一位老师一起上课，临走前霍金把他们一起完成的作业撕得粉碎，扔进了废纸篓里！

有时，霍金这样做是因为他的学识可能比老师更为渊博。不过他也认为，最“酷”的做法是尽量少做点作业就能应付课业。因为霍金非常聪明，所以尽管行为比学校里的大多数学生更恶劣，他也没有受到惩罚。

第三章

不幸的消息

在牛津的第三年，霍金开始有些担忧自己的身体状况。虽然他走路的姿势一直都很笨拙，但现在他会撞到东西。有时他会突然跌倒，系鞋带也有些困难。有一天晚上，他从学校的楼梯上一路跌了下来，当场陷入了昏

迷。霍金刚苏醒过来的时候，压根不记得自己是谁，也不知道自己身处何地。后来他的身体渐渐恢复了，但这是一个警告信号，不过霍金一直选择忽略这个信号。他并没有让父母知道自己的身体出了问题。

霍金忙于参加社交活动，身体也日益笨拙，这一切都可能令他无法集中精力学习，但他从牛津大学毕业时仍然取得了最高荣誉学位。

只有获得一等荣誉学位，霍金接下来才能进入剑桥大学攻读博士学位。哲学博士学位，俗称博士学位，即大学毕业之后攻读科学和其他学科领域获得的学位。

1962 年秋，年仅二十岁的霍金进入剑桥大学三一学院学习宇宙学。宇宙一词有时也指宇宙的秩序。宇宙学是物理学的一个分支，是一门研究宇宙起源及其构成本质的学科。

弗雷德·霍伊尔爵士

对霍金来说，在剑桥大学的学习生涯一开始并不怎么顺利。剑桥大学最顶尖的宇宙学家是一位德高望重的英国科学家，名叫弗雷德·霍伊尔。霍伊尔后来被英国女王封为爵士，称为弗雷德·霍伊尔爵士。霍金希望能师从大名鼎鼎的霍伊尔教授，但学校给他分配的却是另一位教授丹尼斯·夏默。于是霍金在一开始的时候感到相当失望。

丹尼斯·夏默

霍金的宇宙学研究起步也很慢。因为研究宇宙学需要复杂的数学公式，但他在牛津大学学习时并不用功，数学基础没打好，需要迎头赶上。霍金偶尔还是会摔跤。

他变得难以正常说话，有时甚至会口齿不清。

在剑桥的第一个学期结束后，霍金回到家中过圣诞节。在 1963 年的新年聚会上，霍金邂逅了一个名叫简 · 怀尔德的女孩。简比霍金小两岁，对他早有耳闻。

霍金的母亲经常去简的学校接霍金的弟弟妹妹。霍金的父亲曾经清理过她家后院的一大群蜜蜂。但在新年聚会上，霍金和简才进行了第一次交谈。霍金灿烂的笑容、灰色的眼睛和风趣幽默的性格让简倍感喜悦。一周后，在霍金二十一岁的生日派对上，两人又一次畅聊良久。

不过，派对结束后不久，霍金发现他再也无法向父

母隐瞒自己的身体问题了，于是父母带他去看了家庭医生。医生将他送到医院进行检查。

在医院里，医生用注射器针头在霍金身上戳来戳去，采集肌肉样本。他们给他做了各种各样的检查。两周后，霍金和家人终于从医生那里得知了消息，却是一个不幸的消息。

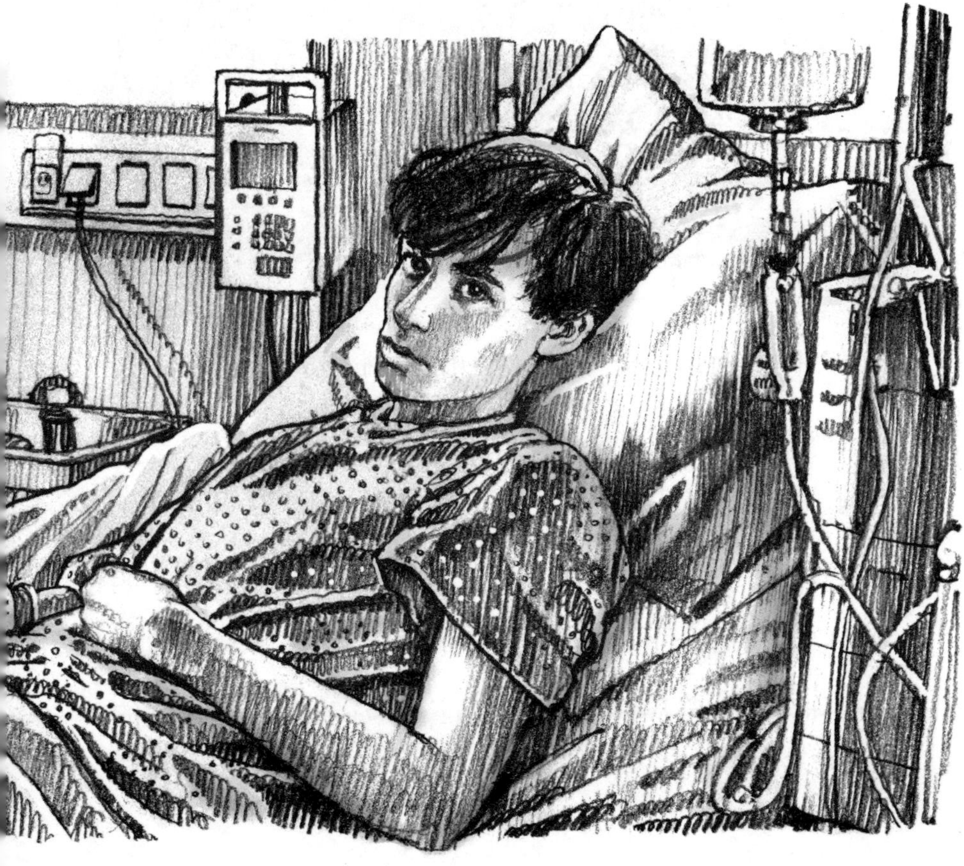

医生确诊霍金患有一种叫肌萎缩侧索硬化的疾病。该病的患者控制身体肌肉的细胞，即运动神经元受到影响。随着病情不断恶化，患者的胳膊、腿、手和脚会越来越不听使唤。很快患者就会完全无法动弹，甚至不能呼吸。这是一种无法治愈的疾病。在美国，该疾病通常被称为卢伽雷氏症（Lou Gehrig’s disease），因为著名的棒球运动员卢·格里克（Lou Gehrig）就因罹患该病离开了人世。

霍金的医生告诉他，他们对此无能为力。医生认为霍金只剩下两年的生命，建议他这两年最好还是回剑桥去。他可以在剑桥大学继续进行研究，攻读博士学位。

霍金非常艰难地接受了这个消息。如果他没法在学校待足够长的时间，找寻到那些问题的答案，那他不确定回到剑桥继续思考宇宙的重大问题还有多大意义。甚至在确诊之前，他就觉得自己并没有什么进步。

卢·格里克（1903—1941）

一垒手卢·格里克是美国职业棒球大联盟历史上最伟大的球员之一。从1923年开始，他效力于纽约杨基队，打了17个赛季，击球率达0.340，全垒打数为493支。卢·格里克7次入选全明星赛，两次被评为美国联盟最有价值球员，并助力杨基队赢得6个世界大赛冠军。

1925年，卢·格里克成为先发球员，每场比赛都会出现在杨基队的首发阵容中。事实上，他的绰号是“铁马”，因为他创下了当时美国职业棒球大联盟的纪录：连续2130场比赛不间断出场！1939年，他被诊断出患有肌萎缩侧索硬化，更是让所有人大为震惊。同年5月的一场比赛之后，他再也没有打过比赛。

1939年7月4日，球队在杨基体育场举行仪式，向卢·格里克致敬。他发表了著名的告别演讲：“过去两周里，想必你们都听闻了我的不幸遭遇。但现在，我想我是这个世界上最幸运的人。”

1939年，卢·格里克入选美国国家棒球名人堂。

1941年，卢·格里克去世，年仅三十七岁。

现在，疾病一定会进一步拖慢他学习的脚步。他甚至无法细想自己能不能活到博士毕业，至少需要三年时间他才能拿到博士学位。

霍金深受打击，十分悲伤。他有时会独自坐在黑暗中听古典音乐。

霍金开始做噩梦，他的朋友和家人都非常担忧。

夏默教授帮忙说服霍金回到学校，于是霍金继续自己在剑桥大学的学业。他有的时候会在周末回一趟家。一天早上，霍金在返程路上的火车站看到了简。她正要去伦敦，而伦敦就在去剑桥的火车沿线上。简知道霍金一直待在医院，但自 1 月份以来，她就没有和霍金说过话。

霍金和简在去伦敦的火车上一路交谈。霍金邀请简跟他约会。他们一起吃了晚餐，看了一场话剧。两人开始频繁见面，很快就坠入了爱河。

第四章

找到目标

用霍金的话说，爱上简给了他“活下去的意义”。和霍金一样，简也有点害羞，同时又很有主见。她也很聪明，很快就要攻读博士学位，研究中世纪的西班牙诗歌。

6月，霍金带简参加了三一学院的5月舞会。5月舞会有点像美国的毕业舞会，但更加豪华。没错，剑桥的5月舞会就是在6月举办！

霍金和简度过了一段美好时光。坠入爱河给了霍金一个继续攻读博士学位的理由。如果他想和简结婚，就必须想办法谋生。为此，他必须完成博士学业。他有生以来第一次开始努力学习。霍金表示：“出乎我意料的是，我发现我喜欢这样努力学习。”

霍金主要研究的是宇宙的起源问题。他想弄清楚从

本质上说，宇宙是一直恒定不变的，还是始于一场“大爆炸”。

霍金不再为师从夏默教授而非霍伊尔教授而感到失望。夏默教授给了他一些很好的建议，对霍金本人的关注肯定也比霍伊尔教授能给的更多。因为霍伊尔教授经常外出做讲座或参加会议。

大爆炸与稳态

霍金刚开始研究宇宙学的时候，科学家们主要从两个方面思考宇宙的起源。他们想知道是否可以通过研究知道宇宙是如何诞生的。一些科学家相信稳态理论，另一些科学家则支持大爆炸理论。

稳态理论认为宇宙无始无终，既没有起源，也没有终结。从任何角度、任何时间看，宇宙都是恒定不变的。即便星系膨胀，相互远离，新的

物质也会填补空隙，令一切保持基本不变。

根据大爆炸理论，时间、空间、质量和能量都源于一个体积极小的点。这个点发生了“爆炸”，宇宙由此产生。自那时起，宇宙一直都在膨胀。

弗雷德·霍伊尔坚信稳态理论。他想出了“大爆炸”这个名字，以此来嘲笑这个他认为愚蠢至极的理论。但这个名字却一直沿用至今。如今，大多数宇宙学家都坚信大爆炸理论，而稳态理论则鲜有人支持。

霍金申请并获得了研究奖学金，这意味着他可以通过做研究获得报酬。找到一份工作之后，霍金也有钱养家糊口了。1964 年 10 月，霍金向简求婚。1965 年 7 月，两人结婚，随后前往美国度蜜月。他们还一起去了纽约的康奈尔大学参加一个物理学会议！

霍金的病情迅速恶化。好消息是，医生一开始预计他只能再活两年时间，但两年后霍金仍然活着。坏消息是，霍金需要拄着拐杖才能行走，有一只手臂也渐渐不听使唤。他连完成博士学位论文都有困难。于是，简帮他打字。

1966年3月，霍金获得应用数学和理论物理学博士学位。同年，他撰写了一篇论文。凭借这篇论文，他获得了亚当斯奖。亚当斯奖是一项大奖，也是剑桥大学最受重视的奖项之一。

简也在继续攻读自己的博士学位。不过，她的大部分时间都花在照顾霍金以及不久后出世的孩子上。1967年，霍金和简的儿子出生，取名罗伯特。1970年，两人的女儿露西也来到了这个世界。

霍金的双手和双腿都渐渐不听使唤。到20世纪60年代末，他甚至没法站在黑板前面，也无法写出很长的

方程式。他需要拄着拐杖才能四处走动。但他一直拒绝坐轮椅。简说："让霍金同意坐上轮椅是一场大战。"到 1969 年，霍金别无选择。往后余生，他只能一直坐在轮椅上。

出乎意料的是，霍金越是行动不便，越是需要依赖他人的照顾，就越有时间思考宇宙的重大问题。

第五章

新的发现

1970年的一天晚上，霍金正准备睡觉时，突然灵光一闪，有了一个想法。好吧，也许并不是灵光一闪。霍金老是开玩笑说自己总是要花很长的时间才准备好睡觉，因此他有足够的时间来思考重大问题。这天晚上，他正在思考黑洞的问题。这时他突然意识到自己正在做的一些研究可以应用到黑洞研究当中。

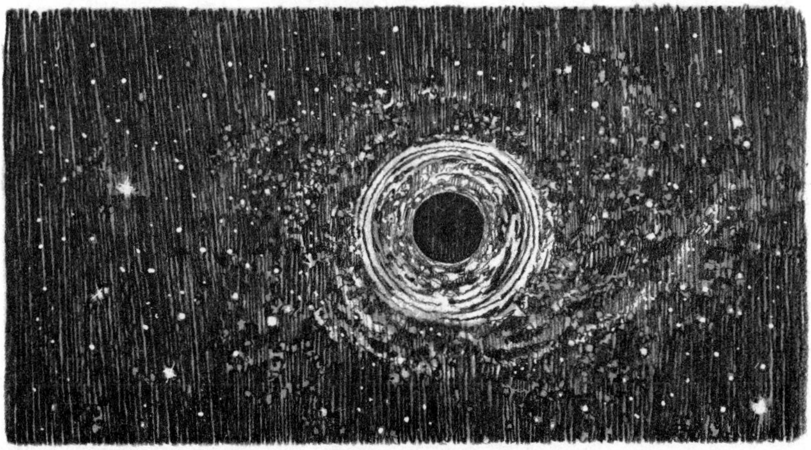

其实黑洞并不是黑色的，也不是真正的洞。它是空间中的一个引力非常强大的区域，大到任何东西都无法从中逃脱，甚至光也不行。

黑洞是有边界的，我们称之为事件视界。任何穿过事件视界的东西都会永远消失。霍金通常会举这个例子来解释：假设你划着独木舟向瀑布驶去，如果你朝相反的方向划得足够快、足够有力，那么你仍然可以逃离瀑布。但是，一旦独木舟靠近瀑布边缘，船就掉进去了，再也没有回头路。

能量可以逃出黑洞的事件视界吗？1974年，霍金发现正能量粒子可以逃离黑洞。这种能量就像为了避免越过瀑布而划桨远离瀑布边缘的独木舟上的人。这一概念最终被称为霍金辐射。这也可以说是霍金最著名的发现。

这一发现意义重大。因为这项发现表明，只有负能量粒子会穿过事件视界到达黑洞内部，而进入黑洞的负能量粒子会消耗黑洞的质量，使得黑洞体积不断缩小。黑洞收缩到一定程度时就会爆炸，将物质重新释放到太空中。

霍金曾说：“黑洞并不像人们曾经认为的那样是永恒的监狱。物质可以逃离黑洞，既可能去到黑洞的外部，也可能进入另一个宇宙。”

然后他开了个玩笑：“所以，如果你觉得自己身处黑洞中，不要放弃，总会有一条出路的。”这是一个玩笑，也是一个深刻的教训。

霍金也许觉得自身的疾病让他陷入了自己的黑洞。但对他来说，出路在于他的思想。即便他的身体一直在慢慢衰竭，但他的思想却从未受到影响。

就在霍金发现霍金辐射的同一年，他担任了加州理工学院的客座教授。

霍金的家人也随他一起搬到加利福尼亚州的帕萨迪纳住了一年。简一个人照顾不过来，急需他人帮助，于是学校安排了一个大学生来帮忙照顾霍金。自那时起，学生们开始帮助照顾霍金。这是一个皆大欢喜的局面：简得到了她需要的帮助，霍金也得到了照顾，而学生则与世界上最聪明的人之一待在一起。1975 年，霍金一家人回到英国，霍金开始在剑桥大学从事教学和研究工作。

20 世纪 70 年代，霍金获得了多个重要奖项和奖章，并于 1977 年晋升，获得“教授”头衔。

接着，在 1979 年，霍金任剑桥大学卢卡斯数学教授。这可以说是霍金职业生涯中最为重要的荣誉。自 1664 年英国国王查理二世设立卢卡斯教授一职以来，以亨利·卢卡斯命名的卢卡斯教授只有十九位！霍金是第十七位。其中最著名的卢卡斯教授是艾萨克·牛顿爵士。

1979 年，霍金和简有了第三个孩子，名叫蒂莫西。与妻子和孩子们一起生活的时候，霍金尽量像个正常人一样。他们会在家里的后院玩耍，孩子们有时还会跳到霍金的腿上坐轮椅。

艾萨克·牛顿爵士（1643—1727）

1665年，二十二岁的艾萨克·牛顿坐在母亲的位于英国乡村的农舍外。他看到一个苹果从树上掉了下来，这引发了他的思考。为什么物体会落地？为什么物体不会飞向天空？答案就是重力！

二十多年后，牛顿提出了三大运动定律。第一定律指出，如果物体处在运动状态，它就会一直保持运动状态，直到有外力迫使它停止；如果物体处在静止状态，它就会一直保持静止状态，直到有外力迫使它运动。第二定律运用数学说明迫使物体运动或停止需要多大的力。第三定律指出，相互作用的两个物体之间的作用力和反作用力总是大小相等，方向相反。

可能对现在的我们来说，牛顿提出的这些概念都是一些基本的概念。但在牛顿那个时代，这些概念都是颠覆性的，是全新的思维方式。

在牛顿的一生中，他在光、颜色和数学方面也有许多发现。他在万有引力和运动定律方面的研究改变了我们对宇宙的思考方式。他是有史以来最具影响力的科学家之一。

霍金一家人去海滩游玩。简把霍金的轮椅推到沙滩上，霍金光着脚，感受飞溅而来的浪花。

不在海边的时候，霍金会坐在轮椅上疯狂转圈，这一点也相当出名。一位访客回忆说，霍金一坐上轮椅，

就猛地转了好几圈，紧接着就把轮椅开得飞快，把助手甩在后面，助手就在后面追赶！

然而，霍金说的话变得越来越难听懂。很多时候，简或者霍金的助手不得不“翻译”他想说的话。1979 年

11 月 16 日，霍金签署了一份协议，履行他作为剑桥大学卢卡斯数学教授的职责。这是霍金最后一次签署自己的名字。从那以后，他再也无法用手握笔写字。这确实是个问题，但霍金总是能妥善处理好自己遇到的种种麻烦。他说过："一个人必须足够成熟，才能意识到生活并不公平。面对这种情况，你只能尽力而为。"

由于霍金无法在纸上写出关于空间和黑洞的物理方程式，他只能在脑海中思考问题，解决问题。他总是在脑海中想象宇宙的运行方式，回答自己思索的重大问题。

第六章

一本人人能读懂的书

霍金有一个梦想，那就是写一本书来解答自己思考的重大问题。但他希望每个人都能读懂这本书，而不是只有科学家能看懂。他想写一本人们在机场的时候可以拿起来翻看的书，人们可以在长途旅行的间隙阅读这本书。毕竟，为什么他的发现要局限于一小部分能像他一样思考的科学家呢？

出版商却不这么认为。霍金想写的是一本关于宇宙运行方式的书，并非旅客们在机场报摊上拿起的那种轻松读物，也不是大多数人在书店随处可买到的书！

要是自己能用日常用语阐明宇宙的运行方式，人们一定会感兴趣，霍金对此深信不疑。于是，他开始努力写书，笔耕不辍。1984 年，他写完了第一章，还找到了一家出版社，对方有意出版他的著作。1985 年，霍金完成了整本书的写作。

霍金开心极了。出版商却并不高兴，因为这本书的用词还是非常专业，并不日常。霍金的理论对大多数人来说仍然晦涩难懂。物理学是一门非常复杂的学科！于是，霍金的编辑把手稿寄回，还提出了修改意见。这在出版界并不罕见。

然而，霍金还没来

得及做任何修改就病倒了。1985 年，霍金在瑞士参加会议，这时他的病情急剧恶化。一辆救护车来到他下榻的酒店，将霍金紧急送往医院。

霍金患的是肺炎。这种疾病会影响肺部，身体健康的人一般都可以痊愈。但对已经患上肌萎缩侧索硬化的霍金来说，这看起来将是一场灾难。医生已经不抱任何希望，但简却坚持认为自己的丈夫可以活下来。简希望霍金能回剑桥接受治疗。医生警告她，如果他们把霍金移走，他可能会死。在简的坚持下，她和霍金回到了英国。

几周后，霍金痊愈了。但是，为了让他能够自主呼吸，而不是需要在瑞士的医院里接上所有管子进行呼吸，医生们不得不给他做了气管切开手术。术后，霍金只能通过喉咙里的一根管子呼吸，而不是通过鼻子和嘴巴。霍金以前说话就很困难了。如今，霍金彻底不能说话了。他无法发出任何声音。

霍金活了下来，但他的生活又面临着新的更大的问题：他的工作怎么办？他该如何与人交流？他怎么可能完成他的书？他无法在纸上写字，也无法自己打字。现在，他甚至不能大声说出这些单词，让别人帮忙打字。他唯一的交流方式就是别人指着拼写板上的字母，他点头或眨眼。这样他要花很长时间才能完成那本书！

对霍金来说，这又是一段艰难的时期。他说，数周的恢复期“是我一生中最黑暗的一段时光”。现在，霍金二十四小时都需要身边有医疗人员照顾。由于护士们无时无刻不在家里，霍金和简几乎没有隐私可言。

日子也许十分艰难，但霍金和简一直怀揣希望。英

国国民健康服务体系及各类慈善机构都愿意为霍金支付昂贵的医疗护理费用。更有价值的帮助来自美国。加利福尼亚州的一位计算机专家给霍金发来了一个名为“均衡器”的程序。这个程序可以在霍金在大学和家里的电脑上运行。通过这个程序，霍金可以点击手中的装置突出显示某些单词或短语。这个装置类似电脑鼠标。点击之后，一个由计算机生成的声音就会说出霍金标出的单词。虽然这远远比不上今天的技术，但仍为霍金提供了一种交流方式。

霍金很快就学会了如何操作这个程序，速度之快让医生和助手都十分惊讶。唯一的缺点就是这个程序的早期版本只允许他每分钟创建约十个单词，语速相当缓慢。不过，霍金开玩笑说：“我的思维也很慢，所以这个程序再合适不过了！”

霍金开始继续完成之前的那本书。虽然过程十分漫长，但他还是完成了对手稿的修改。1988 年，霍金的著作《时间简史》在世界各地出版。

第七章

名人地位

与往常一样，霍金的判断总是正确的。人们确实很想读一本用日常语言写的关于宇宙起源、黑洞及其他科学概念的书。《时间简史》在畅销书排行榜上名列前茅。

到 1988 年底，《时间简史》一跃成为美国最畅销的非小说类图书。该书在英国、法国、德国和意大利等地也成为第一畅销书，并被翻译成数十种语言。《时间简史》甚至因在伦敦《周末泰晤士报》畅销书排行榜上霸榜四年之久而被载入吉尼斯世界纪录！这本书至今仍在印刷，销量超过一千万册。

《时间简史》出版之后，霍

金在世界各地都成了名人。尽管他在科学界已经相当有名，但世界上拥有“名人”地位的物理学家并不多。

霍金应邀向世界各地的观众介绍自己的著作及职业生涯。

霍金是个明星了，他甚至有自己的粉丝俱乐部！

霍金的办公室和家中都摆放着许多霍金与其他名人的合影，包括英国女王伊丽莎白二世、美国总统贝拉克·奥巴马和第一夫人米歇尔·奥巴马以及三位教皇：教皇若望·保禄二世、教皇本笃十六世和教皇方济各。

太空外星人

霍金在剑桥大学有一间办公室，墙上挂了很多名人照片，有一张是他与好莱坞导演史蒂文·斯皮尔伯格的合影。在他们中间窥视的是一个太空外星人，也就是斯皮尔伯格在 1982 年拍摄的电影《E.T. 外星人》中的主角。

霍金对银河系和宇宙起源非常了解，那么他对地球以外的生命有何看法？他相信外星人吗？答案是他相信！霍金在晚年曾说："随着年龄的增长，我比以往任何时候都更加坚信，我们并不孤独。"

20世纪80年代初，在意大利梵蒂冈举办的一次科学家聚会上，霍金见到了教皇若望·保禄二世。霍金当时还能发出声音，尽管他说的话总是难以理解。教皇若望·保禄二世不得不单膝跪在霍金的轮椅旁，以便近距离听到霍金的声音。“情况跟伽利略那时候比真是大不相同了！”另一位与会的科学家说，他还记得伟大的科学家伽利略曾经遭受的不公正待遇。

不幸的是，成为名人并非总是一帆风顺的。出名之后，霍金要经常出差，不停地与人会面，一次又一次地发表演讲。霍金和家人待在一起的时间越来越少。他和简渐行渐远。两人于1990年分居，于1995年正式离婚。

1995年，霍金与伊莱恩·梅森结婚。伊莱恩曾经是照顾霍金的护士之一。两人的婚姻维持了十一年，于2006年离婚。

轮椅

霍金在1969年坐的第一辆轮椅是非常基本的款式。但在晚年，他使用的轮椅堪称高科技奇迹。

霍金可以坐在轮椅上撰写演讲稿、发送电子邮件以及浏览网页。他可以通过Skype（一款网络即时语音沟通工具）与访客进行交流。他甚至可以遥控电视、开关电灯以及开关门。这一切都是通过安装在霍金的眼镜上的传感器实现的。传

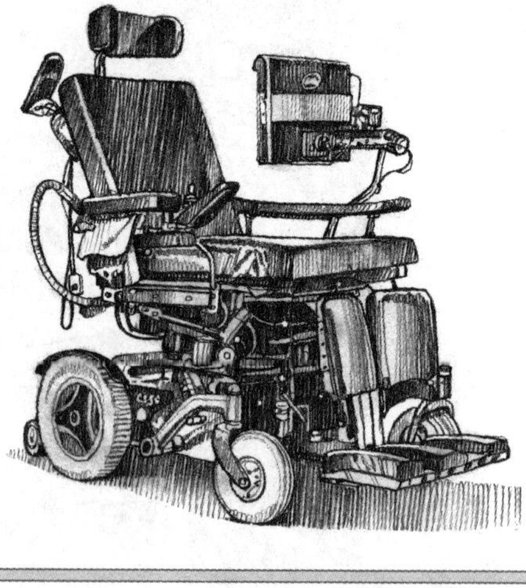

感器能够控制安装在轮椅扶手上的计算机系统。

这台计算机是一台 Windows 平板电脑，屏幕尺寸为十二英寸[1]。霍金眼镜上的传感器能检测到他脸颊肌肉的活动，从而突出显示字母、单词、短语或指令。书面文字通过安装在椅背上的语音合成器（一种能发出声音的电子仪器）翻译成霍金的“声音”。一切都由座椅下方的电池组供电。

① 英寸：英美制长度单位。1 英寸≈ 2.54 厘米。

第八章

人类精神

到 20 世纪 90 年代，霍金已经全球闻名。当然，人们一眼就能认出霍金，因为他一直都坐在轮椅上，而且他是地球上最聪明的人之一。霍金的名气与日俱增。

1991 年，《时间简史》拍成了电影。虽然片名与霍金的畅销书书名相同，但影片主要讲述的是霍金的生活。

在《时间简史》的一次放映现场，演员伦纳德·尼莫伊向在场观众介绍了霍金。尼莫伊曾在科幻电视剧《星际迷航》和多部《星际迷航》电影中扮演斯波克一角。他

伦纳德 · 尼莫伊

发现霍金是《星际迷航》的忠实粉丝后，便帮忙把霍金邀请到《星际迷航：下一代》的片场。制作人邀请霍金出演其中一集时，霍金欣然答应。

此后，霍金经常受邀作为嘉宾出现在电视节目当中。1999 年，霍金首次出现在动画片《辛普森一家》中（当然是以动画的形式），在“他们拯救了莉萨的大脑”一集中出现。

“陨落”

问题：谁是《星际迷航》系列剧集中唯一以自己身份出现的客串明星？

答案：霍金！

在 1993 年播出的《星际迷航：下一代》“陨落”一集中，霍金来到了 24 世纪，与物理学家牛顿、爱因斯坦以及《星际迷航》中的人物“达塔”打了一局扑克牌。

游戏结束时，爱因斯坦确信自己赢了。然而，霍金亮出了自己的牌，表明他才是赢家。“爱因斯坦，你又错了！”霍金咧嘴笑着说。他总是喜欢自己是正确的那一方！

之后，霍金又多次在《辛普森一家》和《飞出个未来》中出演。他在电视喜剧《生活大爆炸》中出演七次，有时只是配音。

霍金与《生活大爆炸》剧组合影

霍金的声音非常独特，有点像机器人，但又有足够的起伏和音调，听起来也很像人声。不过他的声音听起来像美国人！霍金出生在英国，但别忘了，最初的程序是由美国的一位计算机专家发给霍金的。最后，技术的发展使得霍金可以改变电脑的声音。但霍金并不想这么做，因为这个声音已经成为他的一部分。

由于患有肌萎缩侧索硬化长达半个多世纪，霍金的身体已经完全残疾。他的肌肉无法活动。霍金完全依赖他人的照顾。助手们给他喂饭、洗漱、穿衣服、洗澡。他坐轮椅时也得有人帮忙。到 2008 年，霍金甚至无法用手点击电脑上的鼠标。

尽管与更现代的技术相比，霍金的声音听起来可能有些过时，但这个让霍金能够与他人进行交流的程序肯定没有过时。在生命的最后十年里，霍金一直都是用脸颊上的一块肌肉移动电脑上的光标来“说话”。这个先进的程序使用了文字识别技术。智能手机上也有类似的技术。通过这个程序，霍金还可以打开电子邮件、微软

Word 和 Skype 等程序。

如果有一天霍金再也无法移动那块脸颊肌肉，那会发生什么呢？这确实是一个令人担忧的问题。科学家们开始与霍金一起研究一个面部识别程序，甚至尝试将大脑信号转换成语音。这种转换称为脑机接口或 BMI。霍金对脑机接口进行了实验，但进展甚微。虽然脑机接口在霍金有生之年并未实现，但科学家们仍希望在不久的将来能将大脑信号转换成语音。

霍金说过：“因为每个崭新的一天都可能是我生命的最后一天，所以我一直以来的愿望就是充分利用好生命中的每一分钟。”霍金做到了这一点。尽管身患疾病，但他仍然保持积极的生活状态。

2007 年，霍金在美国国家航空和航天局的一架零重力飞机上体验了失重飞行。在航天局专家的帮助下，霍金在空中飘浮、上升、下降，甚至翻转身体。从霍金脸上绽放的笑容就可以看出，他玩得非常开心。

零重力

eroG.com

同年，霍金和他的女儿露西合作，写了《乔治的宇宙 秘密钥匙》一书。这是一本儿童读物，主角是 Cosmos，一台能够帮助人们遨游太空的电脑。随后，该系列的其他四本书陆续出版。

2009 年，美国总统奥巴马授予霍金总统自由勋章，以表彰他对科学的贡献。这是美国授予平民的最高荣誉。

2012年，霍金在伦敦残奥会开幕式上发表演讲，揭开了残奥会的序幕。他对坐在伦敦奥林匹克体育场的选手和观众说：“残奥会意在改变我们对世界的看法。我们

每个人都是与众不同的。世界上本没有正常人或普通人，但我们拥有同样的人类精神。无论生活看起来有多么艰难，总有你能做的事，总有你能取得的成功。”

霍金的生活无比艰难，但他从未失去对成功的强烈渴望。

2014 年，霍金和简·怀尔德的爱情故事被拍摄成电影《万物理论》。

霍金与《万物理论》中的两个明星合影

埃迪·雷德梅因饰演霍金，费莉西蒂·琼斯饰演简。电影临近尾声时，剧中的霍金对简说：“看看我们创造的。”他是说他和简一起组建的家庭，还有一路走来取得的许多成功。

2018年3月14日，在剑桥家中，霍金于睡梦中安详离世，享年七十六岁。从医生预言他活不过二十三岁以来，已经过去了五十多年。直到去世之前，霍金一直都在剑桥大学理论宇宙学中心积极工作，担任研究主任一职。

霍金最重要的成就是什么？是他的科学发现，比如霍金辐射吗？还是他从未让疾病阻碍自己尽情享受生活的脚步的个人精神、英勇无畏的个人经历？抑或是他通过自己最畅销的书向全世界的人解释了艰深的科学概念？

霍金的一生充满了重大问题。在这一生中，他孜孜不倦地寻找正确答案。

斯蒂芬·霍金生平年表

1942 年 — 1 月 8 日，斯蒂芬·霍金出生于英国牛津。
1959 年 — 进入牛津大学学院学习。
1963 年 — 经诊断患有运动神经元疾病，肌萎缩侧索硬化（又称卢伽雷氏症，ALS）。
1965 年 — 与简·怀尔德结婚。
1966 年 — 获得剑桥大学博士学位。
1967 年 — 儿子罗伯特出生。
1970 年 — 女儿露西出生。
1974 年 — 发现“霍金辐射”。
1979 年 — 成为剑桥大学卢卡斯数学教授。
— 儿子蒂莫西出生。
1988 年 —《时间简史》出版。
1991 年 — 关于霍金及其生活的纪录片《时间简史》上映。
1995 年 — 与简·怀尔德离婚，与伊莱恩·梅森结婚。
2006 年 — 与伊莱恩·梅森离婚。
2009 年 — 获得总统自由勋章，是美国平民的最高荣誉。
2012 年 — 在伦敦残奥会开幕式上发表演讲。
2014 年 — 讲述霍金和简爱情故事的电影《万物理论》上映。
2018 年 — 3 月 14 日于英国剑桥离世。

世界大事记

1939 年	德国入侵波兰，第二次世界大战爆发。
1945 年	8 月，美国在日本广岛和长崎投放原子弹，不久，第二次世界大战结束。
1951 年	第一台彩色电视机问世。
1955 年	因拒绝在公共汽车上给白人乘客让座，罗莎·帕克斯在亚拉巴马州的蒙哥马利市被捕。
1961 年	4 月，苏联航天员尤里·加加林成为第一个进入太空的人。
	5 月，艾伦·谢泼德成为第一个进入太空的美国宇航员。
1969 年	美国宇航员尼尔·阿姆斯特朗成为第一个登上月球的人。
1976 年	史蒂夫·乔布斯、史蒂夫·沃兹尼亚克和罗纳德·韦恩共同创办苹果公司。
1997 年	第一部哈利·波特小说在英国出版。
2001 年	9 月 11 日，美国发生恐怖袭击事件，纽约世贸中心遭到摧毁，近三千人丧生。
2008 年	贝拉克·奥巴马当选美国首位非洲裔总统。
2018 年	美国私营企业太空探索技术公司向太空发射“重型猎鹰”运载火箭。

Who Was Stephen Hawking?

When Stephen Hawking was a young boy, he wanted a toy train more than anything else in the world. But he lived in England in the mid-1940s, during World War II. Toy makers weren't making toys at that time. They were too busy helping the war effort. Their factories were being used to help build planes and bombs for soldiers. Toy trains were hard to come by.

So when Stephen was three years old, his father made him a wooden train. But Stephen didn't think of it as a *real* train. He had to push it to make it go. Then Stephen's father managed to find a windup train. After he turned the key, it moved on its own, but it still wasn't the kind of train Stephen wanted.

Stephen was hoping for an electric train with real

moving parts. He wanted to study how the train worked—what made it go and what made it stop. Finally, when he was old enough, he took out all the money he had in his bank account and bought himself an electric train set. That was more like it!

Stephen soon moved on to bigger things. He started building model airplanes. Then he worked on making toy boats. He didn't really care how they looked. Instead, he was more interested in how they worked. Sometimes he took things apart. He wasn't very good at putting them back together, but that didn't matter. He wanted to study how all the different parts worked with one another.

By the time he was a teenager, Stephen started thinking about how even larger things worked—really big things, like the universe, for instance. *How did it start?* he wondered. *Does it get larger? Does it get smaller? Will it ever end?*

Those are big questions! Stephen never stopped asking those big questions. Nothing could stop him. Not even a disease that kept him in a wheelchair for most of his life. Not even losing his ability to speak, and then to move at all.

Instead, he overcame the challenges of his disease and became a physicist. Physics is the study of matter (what all things are made of) and energy. People who study physics take a close look at how matter and energy move through space and time.

Stephen kept thinking about the big questions his entire adult life. He wrote articles and books about black holes, the origin of the universe, and all kinds of things. He was a famous scientist, an important thinker, and an inspiration to people all over the world.

Chapter 1

Beginnings

When World War II began in Europe in 1939, Frank and Isobel Hawking lived in London, England. London was heavily bombed during the war by Germany, which was fighting on the other side. Many parts of the city were destroyed. The Hawkings' home wasn't hit, but one bomb landed just a few houses down the street from theirs.

When Isobel was pregnant with Stephen in the early 1940s, she moved for a time to Oxford, England. It was much safer in Oxford, which is about sixty miles away. Oxford is home to the University of Oxford. There were no soldiers or important factories there, so it was not a target for the Germans.

In the safety of Oxford, Stephen Hawking was born on January 8, 1942. It was exactly three hundred years to the day after Italian physicist Galileo died. Stephen, who grew up to become a physicist, liked to joke that there was some significance to that. But he also admitted that thousands of other babies were born on that same day who didn't grow up to become famous scientists!

Frank Hawking studied medicine in college and became an expert in tropical diseases. He and Isobel lived in the Highgate section of London, where many scientists lived.

Stephen was Frank and Isobel's first child. In 1943, they had a daughter named Mary.

Another daughter, Philippa, was born in 1946. The family adopted a baby boy named Edward when Stephen was fourteen years old.

In 1950, the family moved about twenty miles north of Highgate to Saint Albans. Frank had started an important job at the National Institute of Medical Research in Mill Hill, a

Galileo Galilei (1564–1642)

Galileo Galilei is sometimes called "the father of modern physics." During his lifetime, people believed that heavier objects fell at a faster rate than lighter ones. But Galileo found that objects in motion all fall at the same rate of acceleration.

Galileo was an expert in many subjects. He was an astronomer, a mathematician, a philosopher, and an engineer.

As a Roman Catholic, he angered church leaders by arguing that the Earth orbits the sun; at the time, most people believed the sun traveled around the Earth. In 1633, he was found guilty of heresy, which means going against the teachings of the church. He spent the last nine years of his life jailed in his own home.

town outside London. It was easier for him to commute to work from there.

In Saint Albans, the Hawking family sometimes stood out from their neighbors. Eight-year-old Stephen figured it was because not as many scientists lived in Saint Albans as in Highgate. That was true, but there were probably more things that made the Hawkings stand out.

For instance, they drove around town in an old London taxi from the years before the beginning of World War II. The kids were so embarrassed by the family car that they ducked down in the large spaces in the back seat so their friends wouldn't see them drive by! Everybody knew whose car it was, though.

The Hawking family also bought an old caravan, or horse-drawn wagon. They parked it in a field in a nearby town and used it as a vacation spot. On summer holidays, the kids slept in the caravan and the grown-ups pitched an army tent right next to it.

Life inside the Hawking house wasn't typical, either. There were books everywhere. The children even read at dinnertime.

The bookshelves—and there were many—were packed. Even when it looked like they were full, more books were shoved on top or in front of the original rows.

Not surprisingly, Stephen was somewhat quiet. He played a lot on his own. Sometimes, relatives would find him staring at the sky, thinking big thoughts.

But Stephen was not shy about expressing his opinions, and he made many friends. When his friends came over to the Hawking house, the family would put aside their books at dinnertime and talk instead. His young friends were very surprised at the grown-up topics they discussed, like religion or politics. The Hawking house, Stephen said, "was a place where my mind was constantly challenged."

Chapter 2

School Days

As a youngster, Stephen liked to play board games. However, games such as Monopoly quickly became too boring for his active mind. So he and a friend made up their own board games. Stephen's favorite was a war game that was very complicated. It took hours and hours to play because Stephen included so many rules.

His sister Mary later remembered that Stephen was very competitive.

He always wanted to win at whatever game he played. Draughts (say: drafts) is the English version of checkers. Stephen beat Mary at draughts every time they played—except once. When Mary finally beat him, Stephen quit playing draughts and took up chess. Mary never did beat him at that!

Although Stephen was very smart, he didn't learn to read until he was eight, and he rarely studied in school. He did not do neat work, and his handwriting was terrible. He had little interest in memorizing facts, but he had no trouble grasping concepts and ideas.

In his teenage years, Stephen and his friends built a computer. It was nothing like the laptop computers we have today. It was about the size of a refrigerator. The boys built it out of whatever spare parts they could find, including parts from old clocks.

The computer could solve only the most basic problems. But it was still the late 1950s—Stephen was way ahead of his time!

In fact, Stephen's friends called him "Einstein," after famous physicist Albert Einstein, because he was so brilliant. But Stephen was no Einstein in the classroom. Compared with the others in his grade, he was just an average student. He laughed about it later in his life: "It was, I like to think, a very bright class," he said.

Stephen was often bored in school. Physics came *too* easily for him. The solutions were obvious for someone who was thinking so far ahead. Subjects such as chemistry were much more interesting. In chemistry, it was fun to figure out how different elements worked with one another—how some worked well, and others resulted in a bang!

Both Stephen's mother and father had gone to college at Oxford and hoped that Stephen would go there, too. But because of his average grades at Saint Albans School, there was no guarantee he would be accepted to Oxford.

There was also the question of what he would study in college. Frank Hawking wanted his son to follow in his footsteps in medicine, but Stephen had little interest in biology or in becoming a doctor. He wanted to major in math, but University College at Oxford did not offer it as a major.

So Stephen settled on physics instead.

He wowed the faculty at Oxford with an impressive interview and with an even more impressive written exam for physics—nearly a perfect score! Stephen had been accepted to Oxford.

Stephen was only seventeen when he began his studies at Oxford in the fall of 1959. His classmates immediately could see that he was very smart and really funny. Still, it took him a little while to fit in with the other students, almost all of whom were older—many of them by a couple of years or more.

To be more social, Stephen joined the University College Boat Club in his second year. Although he was skinny and not very strong, he found a place among the larger rowers. He was the coxswain (sometimes shortened to *cox*), the smaller person who sits at one end of the boat to direct the rowers and steer.

It took a little while for Stephen to get the hang of being

University of Oxford

The University of Oxford in Oxford, England, is the world's second-oldest university still in operation. (The oldest, Italy's University of Bologna, began in 1088.) There is no official date for Oxford's beginning, but it is believed to be as early as the year 1096.

Thirty- eight different colleges make up the University of Oxford. Each of the thirty-eight colleges has its own teachers and activities. Stephen Hawking attended University College, which is the oldest of the thirty-eight.

Some of the best scholars in the world have gone to Oxford, including several dozen winners of the Nobel Prize. Many world leaders have attended the university, too, including twenty-seven prime ministers of England and one US president, Bill Clinton, who studied at University College for one year in the late 1960s before attending Yale Law School.

a cox. Because the river Thames is narrow at the town of Oxford, the rowing team competed in "bumping" races. In a bumping race, boats start out an equal distance from each other. They try to go fast enough to bump the boat in front and to keep from being bumped by the boat behind.

In his very first race, Stephen let go of the starting line as he was supposed to, but it got caught in the boat's rudder. (The team immediately was disqualified.) Another time, he somehow managed to direct his boat into a head-on collision with another boat. (Not his fault, he said.) Usually, he brought the boat back in with some damage to it, or to the oars of his teammates. ("My coxing career was fairly disastrous," he admitted.)

Still, Stephen enjoyed being out on the river, with the boat speeding through the water. He made friends among the Boat Club members, who were also impressed by how smart he was and by his sense of humor. "The rowing club also introduced me to one of my favorite pastimes at Oxford:

partying!" he said.

Maybe a little too much partying. After his first year at Oxford, Stephen tended to socialize more than he studied. He later estimated that in his entire three years at University College, he spent about one thousand hours studying. That might sound like a lot, but it works out to less than one hour per day! That's actually very little studying, especially for a challenging school like Oxford, and for a difficult course of study such as physics.

Stephen skipped lectures and developed a reputation that he was difficult to work with. He once sat through a session with a tutor and then, before leaving, tore up the work they had done together and dropped it in a wastebasket!

Sometimes Stephen acted this way because he probably knew more than his tutors did. But he also thought the "cool" thing to do was to get by doing as little work as possible. Because Stephen was so smart, he got away with worse behavior than most students at the university.

Chapter 3

Bad News

Something was starting to concern Stephen in his final year at Oxford. Although he had always had an awkward way of walking, now he was starting to bump into things. Sometimes he stumbled unexpectedly. He had trouble tying his shoelaces. Then, one night, he fell all the way down a staircase at school. He was knocked out. When he came to, he couldn't remember who he was or where he was. Stephen recovered from his fall, but it was a warning sign—one that he chose to ignore. He didn't let his parents know he was having problems.

Stephen's social life and his increasing clumsiness may have kept him from concentrating on his studies, but he still managed to graduate from Oxford with top honors.

A first-class degree was a requirement for Stephen's next step: working toward his doctorate at the University of Cambridge. A doctorate is a PhD, which stands for *doctor of philosophy*. It's a degree awarded in the sciences and other subjects that you work toward after college.

Stephen was only twenty years old when he entered Trinity Hall at Cambridge in the fall of 1962 to study cosmology. The cosmos is the universe, and the word sometimes refers to the order of the universe. Cosmology is the type of physics that tries to understand the origins of our universe and the very nature of what it is made of.

Things didn't start out great for Stephen at Cambridge. The top cosmologist there was a highly respected British scientist named Fred Hoyle. He was later knighted by the queen of England and became known as Sir Fred Hoyle. Stephen hoped to study under the famous Hoyle, but at first was disappointed to be assigned a different professor, Dennis

Sciama (say: shar-ma).

Stephen's study of cosmology started off slowly, too, because it required complex math equations. He hadn't taken enough math courses at Oxford, and he needed to catch up. Stephen was still occasionally tripping and falling. And he was beginning to have difficulty talking normally, even sometimes slurring his speech.

After the first term at Cambridge, he went home for the Christmas break. At a 1963 New Year's party, he met a girl named Jane Wilde. Jane, who was two years younger, already knew who Stephen was. His mother often picked up the younger Hawking children at her school. And his father had once cleaned out a swarm of bees from her family's backyard. But Stephen and Jane talked for the first time at the New Year's party. She was delighted with his wide smile, his gray eyes, and his sense of humor. One week later, they talked at length again at Stephen's twenty-first birthday party.

Not long after that party, though, Stephen found he

couldn't hide his physical problems from his parents any longer, and they took him to see the family doctor. The doctor sent him to be examined at the hospital.

The doctors there poked him with needles to take muscle samples. They gave him many different tests. After two weeks, they finally gave Stephen and his family some news—and it wasn't good.

The doctors determined that Stephen had a type of disease called amyotrophic lateral sclerosis (ALS). For a patient with ALS, the cells that control the muscles of the body, called motor neurons, are affected. As the disease gets worse, a person gradually loses his or her ability to use their arms, legs, hands, and feet. They soon can't move at all, and then it becomes impossible to even breathe. ALS is an incurable disease. In the United States, it is often known as Lou Gehrig's disease, after a famous baseball player who died from it.

Stephen's doctors told him there was nothing they

could do. They figured he had only about two years to live. In the meantime, they said, it was best that he go back to Cambridge. He could continue with his research there and keep working toward his doctorate degree.

Stephen took the news hard. He wasn't sure there was much point in going back to Cambridge and thinking about the big questions of the universe if he wasn't going to be around long enough to discover the answers. He hadn't felt like he was making progress even before the diagnosis. Now, the disease was sure to slow him down more. He couldn't imagine even living long enough to finish his PhD, which was at least a three-year process.

Stephen was shocked and sad. He would sometimes just sit in the dark listening to classical music.

He began having terrible nightmares. His friends and his family worried about him.

Professor Sciama helped convince Stephen to return to Cambridge, and so Stephen went back to his studies. He spent some of his weekends at home. One morning, when he was on his way back to the university, he saw Jane Wilde at the train station. She was heading to London, which was along the train route to Cambridge. Jane knew Stephen had been in the hospital, but she had not spoken to him since January.

Stephen and Jane talked on the train all the way to London, and he asked her on a date. They went to dinner and a play, and they began to see more and more of each other. They fell in love.

Lou Gehrig (1903–1941)

First baseman Lou Gehrig is one of the greatest players in Major League Baseball history. In seventeen seasons with the New York Yankees, beginning in 1923, he batted .340 with 493 home runs. He earned seven All-Star Game selections, was named the American League's Most Valuable Player twice, and helped the Yankees win the World Series six times.

Gehrig was in the Yankees' lineup for every game after he became a starter in 1925. In fact, his nickname was "Iron Horse," because he played in what was then an MLB record: 2,130 games in a row! That made it all the more shocking when he was diagnosed with ALS in 1939. After a game in May of that year, he never played again.

The team honored Gehrig in a ceremony at Yankee Stadium on July 4, 1939. "For the past two weeks, you have been reading about the bad break

I got," he famously told the crowd. "Yet, today, I consider myself the luckiest man on the face of the earth."

Lou Gehrig was inducted into the National Baseball Hall of Fame in 1939. He was only thirty-seven years old when he died in 1941.

Chapter 4

Finding a Purpose

Falling in love with Jane Wilde gave Stephen, in his words, "something to live for." Like Stephen, Jane was a bit shy. And, like Stephen, she had strong opinions. She was very smart, too. She would soon be working toward her own PhD in medieval Spanish poetry.

In June, Stephen took Jane to Trinity Hall's May Ball. The May Ball is sort of like a prom in the United States, but even fancier. And, yes: It was held in June!

Stephen and Jane had a wonderful time. Falling in love gave Stephen a reason to keep working toward his doctorate degree. If he wanted to marry Jane, he had to find a way to earn a living. And to do that, he had to finish his PhD. He started working hard for the first time in his life. "To my surprise," he said, "I found I liked it."

Much of the focus of his research was on the origin of the universe. He wanted to find out if the universe had always been essentially the same, or if it had begun with a "big bang."

Stephen was no longer disappointed that he was studying under Sciama instead of Hoyle. Sciama gave him good advice and more personal attention than Hoyle ever would have. Hoyle was often out of town giving lectures or attending conferences.

Stephen applied for, and received, a research fellowship. That meant he would be getting paid to do research. He had found a job and would now have money to support a family. Stephen proposed to Jane in October of 1964, and they were married in July of 1965. They went to the United States on their honeymoon. Jane and Stephen visited Cornell University in New York to attend a physics conference!

Big Bang versus Steady State

When Stephen Hawking first began working in cosmology, scientists mainly thought about the origin of the universe in two ways. They wanted to know if it came into being in a way that could be studied. Some scientists believed in the steady state theory, and some believed in the big bang theory.

According to steady state, the universe has no beginning and no end. It looks the same from any view and at any time. Even if galaxies expand and pull away from each other, new matter fills in the spaces to keep everything pretty much the same.

According to the big bang theory, time, space, mass, and energy began from a tiny point and "exploded" to create the universe, which has been expanding ever since.

Fred Hoyle, who believed firmly in the steady state theory, came up with the name "big bang" as a way to make fun of something he thought was silly. But the name stuck. Today, most cosmologists believe in the big bang theory, while the steady state theory has little support.

Stephen's ALS was quickly progressing. The good news was that he already had survived longer than the two years the doctors originally talked about. The bad news was that he needed a cane to help him walk, and he was losing strength in one arm. He couldn't even type the paper that he needed to complete his PhD. So Jane typed it for him.

Stephen received his PhD in applied mathematics and theoretical physics in March 1966. That same year, he wrote an essay that earned him a share of a major award called the Adams Prize—one of the most respected awards at Cambridge.

Jane continued working toward her own degree. However, most of her time was spent taking care of Stephen—and soon the couple's children. Stephen and Jane had a son named Robert, who was born in 1967. Their daughter, Lucy, was born in 1970.

Stephen continued to gradually lose the use of his hands and legs. By the late 1960s, he could not stand at a blackboard or write out long equations. He needed crutches to get around. But he resisted the idea of using a wheelchair for as long as he could. “One of the great battles was getting Stephen to use a wheelchair,” Jane said. By 1969, he had no choice. He used a wheelchair for the rest of his life.

In an unexpected twist, the less mobile Stephen became and the more he had to rely on the care of others, the more time he had to think about the big questions of the universe.

Chapter 5

New Discoveries

One night in 1970, an idea came to Stephen in a flash just as he was getting ready for bed. Okay, maybe it wasn't really a flash. As Stephen liked to joke, it took him a long time to get ready for bed, so it gave him plenty of time to think over big questions. On this night, he was thinking about black holes, and he had a sudden realization: Some of the work he was doing could be applied to black holes.

A black hole is not really black and not really a hole. It's an area in space with gravity so strong that nothing—not even light—can escape.

The boundary of a black hole is called the event horizon. Anything that crosses the event horizon is lost forever.

Stephen liked the example of someone paddling in a canoe, heading toward a waterfall. If the person paddles fast and strong enough in the opposite direction, he or she can still get away from the waterfall. But once the canoe falls over the edge, it cannot go back up the waterfall.

Could energy escape the event horizon of a black hole? In 1974, Stephen found that it could—in the form of positive energy. That energy is like the person in the canoe who paddles away from the edge of the waterfall to avoid going over it. The concept eventually became known as Hawking radiation. It is perhaps the discovery Stephen is best known for.

This was a big deal because it showed that the only energy that went over the event horizon and into the black hole was negative energy, and that could shrink the hole. When the shrinking hole reached a certain point, it would explode, releasing matter back into space.

Stephen said that black holes "are not the eternal prisons

they were once thought. Things can get out of a black hole, both to the outside, and, possibly, to another universe."

And then he made a joke, but one with a serious lesson: "So, if you feel you are in a black hole, don't give up. There's a way out."

Stephen may have felt as if his disease put him in his own personal black hole. But for him, the way out was through his mind. Even though his body continued to slowly break down, his mind was never affected.

The same year Stephen discovered Hawking radiation, he worked as a visiting professor at the California Institute of Technology.

His family moved with him to Pasadena, California, for one year. Jane needed more and more help with Stephen, so they brought along a university student to help take care of him. From then on, students helped care for Stephen. That was a good situation all around: Jane got the help she needed, Stephen was cared for, and the student spent time with one of the smartest people in the world. The family returned to England in 1975, and Stephen began a job teaching and researching at Cambridge.

Stephen won several major awards and medals in the 1970s, and earned a promotion with the title of "professor" in 1977.

Then, in 1979, he became the Lucasian Professor of Mathematics at Cambridge. It might have been the most important honor of his career. There have been only nineteen Lucasian Professors—named after Henry Lucas—since England's King Charles II established the position in 1664! Stephen was number seventeen. The most famous Lucasian Professor was Sir Isaac Newton.

In 1979, Stephen and Jane had their third child, Timothy. Stephen tried to live as normal a life as he could with his wife and children. They played in the backyard of their home, with the kids sometimes hopping into Stephen's lap for a ride on the wheelchair.

Sir Isaac Newton (1642–1727)

In 1665, twenty-two-year-old Isaac Newton sat outside his mother's farmhouse in the English countryside. He watched an apple fall from a tree, and that got him thinking. Why do objects fall to the ground? Why don't they fall up? The answer: gravity!

More than twenty years later, Newton published his three laws of motion. The first law says that if something is moving, it will keep moving until something makes it stop; if it is still, it will remain still until something makes it move. The second law uses math to show how much force is needed to make something go or stop. The third law says that "for every action, there is an equal and opposite reaction."

Newton's concepts might seem basic to us now. But in his day, they were a whole new way of thinking.

In his lifetime, Newton also made many discoveries about light, color, and math. His work on gravity and the laws of motion changed the way we think about the universe, and he is one of the most influential scientists of all time.

They went to the beach. Jane rolled Stephen's wheelchair onto the sand so the waves could splash at his bare feet.

When they weren't at the beach, Stephen developed a reputation for zipping around wildly in his wheelchair. One visitor recalls him spinning around in circles several times the moment he was first placed in the chair, then taking off with his assistant running behind, trying to catch up!

However, it was getting very difficult to understand Stephen when he talked. Often, Jane or one of Stephen's helpers had to "translate" what he was trying to say. On November 16, 1979, Stephen signed an agreement to fulfill his duties as the Lucasian Professor of Mathematics at Cambridge. It was the last time he ever signed his name. After that, he could no longer use his hands to write. That was a problem, but he always made the best of his troubles. "One has to be grown up enough to realize that life is not fair," he once said. "You just have to do the best you can in the situation you are in."

Because Stephen couldn't write equations about the physics of space and black holes, he had to think problems through in his mind to solve them. He relied on visualizing the way the universe worked to answer his big questions.

Chapter 6

A Book for Everyone

Stephen dreamed of writing a book about the answers to his big questions. But he wanted it to be a book that everyone could read and understand, not just scientists. He wanted to write a book that people could pick up at the airport, say, and read on a flight to a faraway place. After all, why should his discoveries be limited to the small group of scientists who could think like him?

Publishers weren't so sure. A book about how the universe works wasn't the kind of light reading travelers picked up at airport newsstands. It wasn't the kind of reading most people picked up at bookstores anywhere!

But Stephen really believed that people would be

interested in his topic if he could explain it in everyday language. So he began working very hard at writing his book. By 1984, he had finished the first chapter, and he found a publisher who was interested. The next year, he finished writing the rest of the book.

Stephen was happy. The publisher was not. The language was still very scientific, and his theories were still too hard for most people to understand. Physics is a very complex subject! So his editor sent Stephen's manuscript back to him with suggestions for fixes. That's not unusual in the world of publishing.

However, Stephen got sick before he could make any of the corrections. While at a conference in Switzerland, in 1985, he became very ill. An ambulance came to his hotel and rushed him to the hospital.

Stephen had pneumonia—an illness that affects the lungs and is usually treatable in healthy people. But for Stephen, who was already very sick with ALS, it looked as if it would be a disaster. Doctors gave up any hope of saving him. But Jane did not. She wanted him to return to Cambridge for treatment. The doctors warned her he could die if they moved him. Jane insisted, and she and Stephen returned to England.

After several weeks, Stephen recovered. But in order for him to breathe on his own, without all the tubes he had been hooked up to in the hospital in Switzerland, they had to perform a surgery called a tracheotomy (say: TRAKE-ee-AH-toe-mee). After his tracheotomy, Stephen breathed only through a tube in his throat instead of through his nose and mouth. He already had trouble speaking before. Now Stephen would never be able to talk on his own again. He had no voice.

Stephen was alive, but there were new and bigger questions in his life: What would he do about work? How would he communicate with people? How could he possibly finish his book? He couldn't write it on paper. He couldn't type it himself. Now he couldn't even speak the words out loud for someone else to type. The only way he could communicate was by nodding his head or blinking when someone pointed to the letters on a spelling board. It would take forever to complete a book that way!

It was another tough time for Stephen. The many weeks of recovery "were the darkest of my life," he said. Now he needed medical care around the clock. And with nurses around all the time, there would be little privacy for Stephen and Jane.

Times may have been difficult, but Stephen and Jane never gave up hope. Britain's National Health Service and different charities agreed to help pay for Stephen's costly care. Even more valuable help came from the United States. A computer expert in California sent Stephen a program called Equalizer that would work on Stephen's computers at the university and at home. In Equalizer, Stephen could highlight certain words or phrases by clicking a device he held in his hand. It was similar to a computer mouse.

A computer-generated voice then spoke the words he had highlighted. It was a long way from today's technology, but it gave Stephen a way to communicate.

Stephen's doctors and assistants were amazed at how quickly he learned the program. The only downside was that the early versions of the software allowed him to create only about ten words per minute. That is a slow rate of speech. But, Stephen joked, "I think slowly, so it suited me quite well!"

Stephen was back in business. Although it was a long process, he finished the corrections to his manuscript. And in 1988, his book, called *A Brief History of Time*, was published around the world.

Chapter 7

Celebrity Status

As usual, Stephen was right. People really did want to read a book about the origins of the universe, black holes, and other scientific concepts written in everyday language. *A Brief History of Time* zoomed up the best-seller lists.

By the end of 1988, it was the top-selling nonfiction book in the United States. It also reached number one in places such as Britain, France, Germany, and Italy, and was translated into dozens of languages. It even made it into *Guinness World Records* for staying more than four years on the *Sunday Times* of London best-seller list! The book is still in print today, and has sold more than ten million copies.

A Brief History of Time made Stephen an international

celebrity. He was already very well-known in the scientific community, but there aren't many physicists in the world who have "celebrity" status.

Stephen was asked to give talks about his book and his career to audiences all around the world.

He was a star. He even had his own fan club!

In his office and at his home, there were many pictures of Stephen with other famous people, including Queen Elizabeth II, President Barack Obama and First Lady Michelle Obama, and three different popes: Pope John Paul II, Pope Benedict XVI, and Pope Francis.

Stephen met Pope John Paul II at a gathering of scientists at the Vatican in Italy in the early 1980s. Stephen still had his voice then, although he was often difficult to understand. Pope John Paul II had to get down on one knee beside Stephen's wheelchair to get close enough to hear. "Things certainly have changed since Galileo!" another scientist at the meeting said, remembering how unfairly the

Space Aliens

One of the photos of famous people on the wall of Stephen Hawking's office at Cambridge shows him with Hollywood director Steven Spielberg. Peering between them is a space alien, the title character in Spielberg's 1982 film *E.T.: The Extra-Terrestrial*.

With all Stephen Hawking knew about our galaxy and the origins of the universe, what did he think about life beyond Earth? Did he believe in aliens? Yes! "As I grow older, I am more convinced than ever that we are not alone," he said late in his life.

The Chair

Stephen's first wheelchair in 1969 was very basic. But in his later years, he used a chair that was a high-tech marvel.

From his chair, Stephen could write speeches, send e-mails, and browse the web. He could talk to visitors and communicate over Skype. He could even operate the TV, turn the lights on and off, and open and close doors. It was all done with a sensor attached to his glasses. The sensor controlled a computer system mounted on the arm of his chair.

The computer was a Windows tablet PC with a twelve-inch screen. The sensor on his glasses detected movement in the cheek muscle Stephen twitched to highlight letters, words, phrases, or commands. Written words were translated into Stephen's "voice" by a synthesizer—an electronic instrument that produces sound—mounted on the back of the chair. Everything was powered by a battery pack kept under the seat.

church had treated that great scientist.

Unfortunately, being a celebrity wasn't always easy. It meant lots of traveling, constantly meeting with people, and giving speech after speech. Stephen began spending less time with his family. He and Jane drifted apart. They separated in 1990 and officially divorced in 1995.

That same year, Stephen married Elaine Mason. She had been one of the nurses who took care of him. Stephen and Elaine were married for eleven years before divorcing in 2006.

Chapter 8

The Human Spirit

By the 1990s, Stephen was famous around the world. He was, of course, instantly recognizable because he was never out of his wheelchair, and he was one of the smartest people on the planet. And his fame was still growing.

In 1991, *A Brief History of Time* was made into a movie. Although it had the same title as Stephen's best-selling book, it was mostly about his life.

At one showing of *A Brief History of Time*, the actor Leonard Nimoy introduced Stephen to the people watching. Nimoy had played the character Spock in the science-fiction television show *Star Trek* and several *Star Trek* movies. When he found out that Stephen was a big fan of the show, he helped get Stephen invited to the set of *Star Trek: The Next Generation*. And when the makers of the show asked him to appear on an episode, Stephen said yes.

After that, Stephen was often asked to appear as a guest on TV shows. In 1999, he first showed up (in animated form, of course) on *The Simpsons* in an episode called "They Saved Lisa's Brain." Stephen went on to perform in several more episodes of *The Simpsons*, and also on *Futurama*. He made seven appearances in the television comedy *The Big Bang Theory,* sometimes only in voice.

Stephen's voice was very distinctive. It was a little robotic, but with enough rise and fall and tone to make it sound human, too. But it also sounded American! Stephen was born in England, but, remember, the original software was sent by a computer expert in the United States. Eventually, technology allowed Stephen to change his computer's voice. But he didn't want to. It had become part of who he was.

"Descent"

Q: Who is the only guest star to appear as himself or herself on an episode of any *Star Trek* series?

A: Stephen Hawking!

In a 1993 episode of *Star Trek: The Next Generation* called "Descent," Stephen traveled to the twenty-fourth century to play a game of poker with fellow physicists Sir Isaac Newton and Albert Einstein, as well as *Star Trek*'s own character Data.

At the end of the game, Einstein was certain he had won. However, Stephen revealed his cards to show he had the winning hand. "Wrong again, Albert!" Stephen said with a large grin on his face. Stephen still loved being right!

Because he had had ALS for more than half a century, Stephen' s body was completely disabled. His muscles no longer worked. He was totally reliant on the care of others. He was fed and cleaned and dressed and bathed by helpers. He needed someone to push his wheelchair. By 2008, he couldn't even use his hand to click the mouse on his computer.

But while his voice may have sounded a bit out of date compared with more modern technology, the software that allowed Stephen to communicate sure wasn't. Over the final ten years of his life, Stephen "spoke" by using a single cheek muscle to move the cursor on his computer. The advanced software used text recognition, sort of like the technology on a smartphone. It also allowed Stephen to open programs such as e-mail, Microsoft Word, and Skype.

What would have happened if one day Stephen could no longer move that cheek muscle? It was a real concern. Scientists began working with him on facial recognition software, and even on trying to convert brain signals into speech. This conversion is called brain-machine interface, or BMI. Stephen experimented with BMI, but made very little progress. Although it did not happen in Stephen's lifetime, scientists hope to translate brain signals into speech in the near future.

"Because each new day could be my last," Stephen once said, "I have developed a desire to make the most of each and every minute." He did that by maintaining an active life despite his disease.

In 2007, he experienced weightlessness on NASA's zero-gravity aircraft. With the help of NASA experts, he floated, rose, dipped, and was even spun around. The grin on his face gave away what a good time he had.

That same year, Stephen and his daughter, Lucy, wrote a children's book. *George's Secret Key to the Universe* featured a computer called Cosmos that helps people travel into outer space. Four other books in the series followed.

In 2009, President Barack Obama presented Stephen with the Presidential Medal of Freedom for his contributions to science. It's the highest US honor awarded to civilians.

In 2012, Stephen helped launch the Paralympic Games in London with a speech at the opening ceremony. "The Paralympic Games are all about transforming our perception of the world," he told the competitors and the spectators at London's Olympic Stadium. "We are all different. There is no such thing as a standard or run-of-the-mill human being, but we share the same human spirit. However difficult life may seem, there is always something you can do and succeed at."

Stephen's life was incredibly difficult, but he never lost his intense desire to succeed.

In 2014, the love story of Stephen and Jane Wilde was made into the movie *The Theory of Everything*.

Eddie Redmayne played Stephen, and Felicity Jones played Jane. Near the end of the movie, Stephen's character tells Jane's character, "Look what we've made." He meant the family they built, but also the many other successes along the way.

On March 14, 2018, Stephen died peacefully in his sleep at home in Cambridge. He was seventy-six. It had been more than fifty years since doctors predicted he wouldn't live beyond age twenty-three. Until his death, he was actively working at Cambridge as Director of Research at the Centre for Theoretical Cosmology.

What was Stephen Hawking's most important accomplishment? Was it his scientific discoveries, such as Hawking radiation? Was it his heroic personal journey, never letting his disease keep him from living life to its fullest? Or was it explaining difficult scientific ideas to people all over the world through his best-selling book?

Stephen Hawking's life was full of big questions. And throughout it, he worked tirelessly to come up with the right answers.

Timeline of Stephen Hawking's Life

1942	Stephen Hawking is born on January 8 in Oxford, England.
1959	Enters University College, Oxford.
1963	Is diagnosed with motor neuron disease ALS (Lou Gehrig's disease).
1965	Marries Jane Wilde.
1966	Completes his PhD at the University of Cambridge.
1967	Son Robert is born.
1970	Daughter, Lucy, is born.
1974	Discovers what is now known as "Hawking radiation".
1979	Becomes the Lucasian Professor of Mathematics at the University of Cambridge.
	Son Timothy is born.
1988	*A Brief History of Time* is published.
1991	*A Brief History of Time*, a documentary film about Stephen and his life, is released.
1995	Divorces Jane Wilde and marries Elaine Mason.
2006	Divorces Elaine Mason.
2009	Is awarded the Presidential Medal of Freedom, the United States' highest civilian honor.
2012	Officially opens the Paralympic Games in London.
2014	*The Theory of Everything*, a movie about Stephen and Jane's love story, is released.
2018	Dies on March 14 in Cambridge, England.

Timeline of the World

1939	Germany invades Poland, and World War II begins.
1945	In August, atomic bombs are dropped on the Japanese cities Hiroshima and Nagasaki by the United States, leading to the end of World War II.
1951	The first color TV is sold.
1955	Rosa Parks is arrested in Montgomery, Alabama, for refusing to give up her seat on a bus to a white passenger.
1961	In April, Soviet cosmonaut Yuri Gagarin becomes the first person to travel into space.
	In May, US astronaut Alan B. Shepard Jr. becomes the first American in space.
1969	American Neil Armstrong becomes the first person to walk on the moon.
1976	Steve Jobs, Steve Wozniak, and Ronald Wayne start Apple Computer Inc.
1997	The first Harry Potter novel is published in the United Kingdom.
2001	On September 11, terrorist attacks in the United States destroy the World Trade Center in New York City and kill almost three thousand people.
2008	Barack Obama is elected the first African American president of the United States.
2018	Privately owned company SpaceX launches its Falcon Heavy rocket into space.

Bibliography

*Fortey, Jacqueline. Great Scientists. New York: DK Publishing, 2007.

Hawking, Jane. Travelling to Infinity: My Life with Stephen. London: Alma Books, 2007.

*Hawking, Lucy, and Stephen Hawking. George's Secret Key to the Universe. New York: Simon & Schuster Books for Young Readers, 2007.

Hawking, Stephen. My Brief History. New York: Bantam Books, 2013.

Hawking, Stephen W. The Illustrated Theory of Everything: The Origin and Fate of the Universe. Beverly Hills, CA: Phoenix Books, 2003.

*Senker, Cath. Stephen Hawking. Chicago: Heinemann-Raintree, 2016.

White, Michael, and John Gribbin. Stephen Hawking: A Life in Science. New York: Dutton, 1992.

*Books for young readers